You should have seen

just what I heard

Mike Rogers

You should have seen just what I heard

Poems

© 2023 Mike Rogers

All rights reserved. No part of this publication may be reproduced, stored in a retrieval system or transmitted in any form or by any means, electronic, mechanical, photocopying, recording or otherwise without the express written permission of the publisher except for the use of brief quotations in a book review.

ISBN 979-8-218-04085-7

Mike Rogers
harpman9@gmail.com
https://www.harmonicaworkshops.com

10 9 8 7 6 5 4 3 2 1

Dedication

To Joseph and Marjorie Rogers, for all that they do for us every day.

Contents

Acknowledgments — xi

I GROWING PAINS — 1

In Time of War — 2
Pay Day — 3
The Boxer — 4
Smart Pill *(A childhood memory)* — 5
Sargasso Sea — 6
The Smell of Coal — 8
February Snow — 9
Gauntlet — 10
Bubble — 12
Horseshoe Pier — 14
Friends *(For Richie)* — 16
At Seventeen — 17
Straw — 19

II BIG MUDDY — 21

First Date — 22
John Deere School — 23
River Rat — 24
Mississippi Dip — 26
Ralphie — 28

III PANES IN MAINE — 29

Beach Rose — 30

Mousam River	31
Hunters	32
Flagpole	33
King of the Dump	34
Renaissance Maine	36
Photograph	37
Empathy	38
(for Bev)	38
Fort Foster	39
Wagon Wheel	40
Autumn Flight	42
Leaf	43
Fryeburg Fair	44
May Day	46
Lean On Me	49
Congress Square	50
In the Vernacular	51
Painted Lady Morning	52
Cornucopia Lost	53

IV VIEW FROM THE ZOO — 55

Zoo Keeper	56
Big Red	58
A Cruel Cut	60
Canned Heat	62
Magician	64

V ISLAND TIME — 67

Christoforo	68
Witch Baby	70

Bahama Nights	71
Island Road	72
House on Fox Hill	73
Night Drop	75

VI MASON DIXON   77

Bell Ringer	78
For a Pear	80
Sunnyland or Bust	82
Different Worlds	83
Family Matter	84

VII MUSIC GOES ROUND AND ROUND   85

Sonny Terry	86
In the Zone	88
Music Man	89
Audition	90
First Night 2000	92
Mistake	93
Sittin' In	94
Through a Glass Darkly	95

VIII OUTSIDE THE CIRCLE   97

Otto	98
Acrobat Man	99
Ouida	100
Taboo	101
Star on Loan	102
In His Eyes	103
Uptown Threads	104
Vision of Loveliness	105

ix

Just a Closer Walk	106
Stick Man	108

IX SUNSET — 109

Evening Ritual	110
Hourglass	112
Vigil	113
Year of the Orphan	114

X SNAPSHOTS — 115

Tandem Cycling	116
Migrant Birds Over A Cathedral	116
Braille On The A.T.M.	116
Winning the Lottery	116
Gross Neglect	116
National Security	116
TV Reality Shows	116
Free Performance	116
Enigma	117
Jerusalem Swings	118
Down to Galilee	120
Before a Fall	121
Lost in Space	123

Acknowledgments

I'd like to thank the following people for their assistance with this undertaking:

My beautiful wife Beverly, who has shared my life's adventures for the past 58 years, spent long hours editing the poems and suggesting revisions. You are the best part of me.

Our "daughter" Taylore Dawn Kelly used her amazing talents to design the cover and illustrate this book. She also persistently urged me to publish these works. You are something else, kidlet.

Dawn Boyer, who beautifully designed and laid out the interior of the book. I am thankful for her publishing know-how.

John Perrault, friend for over fifty years and a former Portsmouth, NH, Poet Laureate has been there to answer literary questions and occasionally critique verses for me.

Barbara London, another long-time friend, read and discussed revisions to some of my work. She is a wonderful writer of verse.

You two are my "besties."

Special thanks to well-known poet Wesley McNair, who saw potential in my writing and inspired me to take my work seriously.

Lastly, I wish to thank the editors of the following publications where the poems listed below, some in slightly different form, first appeared:
"Otto," *The Anthology of New England Writers*, 2001
"Pay Day," *Northern New England Review*, 2004
"Big Red" and "Canned Heat," *The New Hampshire Gazette*, 2004

I
Growing Pains

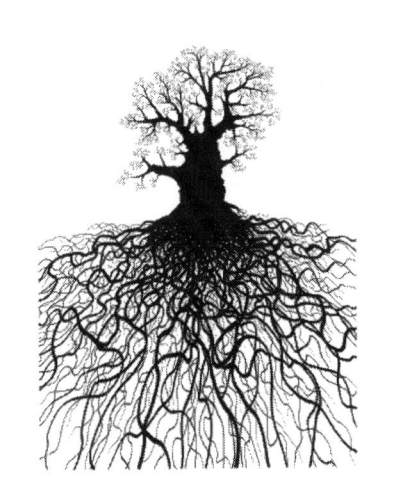

In Time of War

Her hand, darker in hue
than the rolling surf,
but lighter than the sand,
enveloped my own small hand.

Each day, Mother brought me here
to walk among the soldiers,
standing watch for signs
of the unseen enemy.

Gentle thunder of pounding waves
covered the city sounds
of angry horns, sirens,
growling diesel engines that boiled up
just over the hill.
Off-shore winds
kept the smoke of battle
far out to sea.

This world of greens and blues
and shades of tan
is part of me.
I always keep it
close at hand.

Pay Day

The bedroom door groans in protest
from the gentle push
that swings it inward.
Dirty light filters through sheer lace curtains,
falls on the figure
lying across the iron bed.

A crumpled, brown fedora
shrouds swollen features.
One arm sheathed in sodden overcoat
hangs limp, fingertips curled
just above the bedside rug.
Booted feet sag left and right
and tiny mounds of unstamped snow
slide down, to stain the coverlet.

Tavern odors rise up,
from clothes, mouth, body.
Two sounds… his snores
and my mother's quiet weeping…
pull against each other,
pull so hard, almost to   breaking.

The Boxer

"You will run
and I will drive the car, behind.
This is how you train
If you want to be a boxer,"
My father told me
when I was four years old.
But,
I never did.

To bring harm to another being
was, is not in me.
What a constant disappointment
I must have been.

The body changed, is changing still.
It shakes, twists, bucks wildly
to release the man
but the child remains, wedged,
arms and legs spread,
pushing against the inner walls
of the mind.

Mike Rogers

Smart Pill
(A childhood memory)

My little bus has one seat
on the top.
I straddle it,
push with my feet
as I head down the walk.

Out on Pacific Coast Highway
fat-fender cars race along
pushing warm summer breezes aside
to push against me.

On the green, grassy strip
between sidewalk and road,
two older neighborhood boys point down
to the small, dark mound,
coiled like a serpent,
there, on the ground.

"It's a candy bar
take it and see."
There is a similarity, I guess
but green-bottle flies atop the mess
give it away.
Don't think I'll stay
around here today.

Sargasso Sea

Display windows dropped uniform squares of light
like huge pats of oleomargarine,
along the grainy, night-grayed strip of sidewalk
in front of Bullock's Department Store.

We launched ourselves
through revolving, glass doors
allowing time for the extra spin-around,
into a kaleidoscope of color and shape,
scents: perfumes, salted nuts,
new carpet, rubber tires.
sounds: music, footsteps,
rolling boil of multiple conversations.

"Stay together and don't touch anything!"
My mother's command.
We bolted for the shoe department.
Slanted shelves held wingtips, stiletto heels,
high-top tennis shoes, penny loafers,
stuffed with amputated, wooden feet.
The oldest, always first,
I push my U.S. Keds into the slots,
bent to press my face against the viewing glass,
to let my gaze drift, through chartreuse mist,
until it came to rest
on the alabaster bones
of my own feet.

Where now, those magic boxes?
Perhaps in some sealed vault,
keeping company with stacks of asbestos tile
and barrels of DDT.
And what of yesterday's child?
Set loose, by trusting parents
to bathe his feet
in the Sargasso Sea.

The Smell of Coal

The smell of burning coal
drifts into the nostrils,
conjures up a city street.

Red bricks streaked with black dirt,
a rusty sidewalk
stretches to the corner.
Along its curb,
frosted garbage cans stand ready
to do battle
with large, dull-colored automobiles
whose rounded fenders paw the pavement
in anticipation.

Rubber tires roll through slushy, gray snow
and the sizzling sound
bounces off cement walls
that rise to meet the winter sky.
The air numbs my cheeks
and makes
the tops of my ears itch.
I am five years old again
and life is an adventure.

February Snow

It comes late, the first big snow
falling unopposed, through windless sky,
to overpower complacent fields.
The woods out back, a freeze frame,
caught in black and white silence.

In this moment, a little boy
holds the glass ball,
turns it in his hands,
watches the imitation flakes
swirl around and descend
upon a tiny Alpine village.

Gauntlet

Prospect Avenue has no sidewalks.
Dirt paths, trimmed with weeds
outline the street, on both sides.
Four older boys block the way,
consume you with their smiles,
circle to cut off retreat.

They ask, "Where you think you're going?"
A fist steals away breath
another drives your folded body down
to land on cold, unyielding ground.
Taunting laughter floats overhead.
It holds no meaning for you
as air is forced back into lungs.

Four sets of feet move away.
You rise to hands and knees,
hear a distant voice say,
"Bobby, he called you a bastard!"
A high-top tennis shoe,
black with white ankle circle,
U.S. Keds
arcs back, then forward.
The rubber coated toe sends stinging pain
through your rib cage.

Sounds of footsteps grow faint,

replaced by silence.
The stone is there, watching,
just in front of your watery eye,
the stone that watches passing travelers,
watched the first Americans,
perhaps watched Father Junipero Serra
on his coastal journey
to convert the first Americans.

The little stone lies so close.
You see the pitted surface,
craters of a tiny planet
in a dusty universe
where one could run
to escape the savages
that roam, unconstrained,
through a childhood jungle.

Bubble

Like an obedient dog,
it comes when called,
this mental postcard,
moment of pure serenity
that belongs forever
to a ten-year-old child.

A cloudless morning,
perfect Saturday sunshine
warms the body,
but leaves no sweat.

You lie face up,
head pointed downhill
on the long, gentle slope
of a large, vacant lot.

A tiny, single-engine plane
hangs
in the blue wedge of sky
between turned out, shoeless feet.
Distant hum of engine
soothes,
like pudding on the tongue.

You are a raft,
afloat

In a sea of grass.
No point of departure,
no ports of call,
no destination.

A bubble in time,
This place,
where you may visit,
but never stay
for long.

Horseshoe Pier

Walk along the esplanade,
step into the penny arcade.
Stereopticons,
slots for pennies, take a glance.
pinball games,
drop a nickel, take a chance.

Upstairs, in the roller rink,
derby queens dressed in pink,
mirror ball lights up the floor.
Down the stairs and out the door.

Waves roll and slap
against the pilings.
That sound
always gets me smiling.
Seagulls cry
up in the sky.
That sound
always makes me high.

Fried jumbo shrimp
in a paper cup,
was enough
to fill me up.
Candy apple on a stick,
I'd eat enough

to make me sick.

Old men fishing by the railing
black cigars, they don't inhale 'em.
Pretty girls, along the beach.
Now, it's gone,
just out of reach.

Fire took it all
away from here,
But in my mind
I still can see
that horseshoe pier.

Friends
(For Richie)

He picked up the phone
and we were there,
in the old Chevy
jolted backward over forty years
cruising Highway 101.

In the spring, we met again…
to laugh
to fish, swap lies,
talk until we rounded off
the jagged edge of adolescence.

Sometimes, we stumble over gifts
left for us to find.
Within two years
my rugged friend was gone,
brought down
by such a tiny parasite
So now I wait
before we put the coffee on
once more.

At Seventeen

A 1947 wood trimmed Chrysler station wagon,
interior finished off in chrome and leather,
yesterday's luxury ride waits at the corner.
Twice a week, in early evening
Jim drives us to the horseshoe pier
that curves around Redondo's waterfront.

Park by the Penny Arcade.
Climb the stairs to the coffeehouse.
A sign in the front window reads:
    "Iconoclast
    Live Music tonight"
Open the door and step down.

One dollar buys a pot of tea.
The folksinger laments, finger picks his guitar.
"They call the wind Mariah."
On vinyl, Lenny Bruce
crucifies all things sacred.
Ferlinghetti recites
about a dog with a tail
and a tail to tell it with.

Jim resembles the sad-eyed beatnik bird
in Pogo's comic strip.
Richard looks, smiles, and laughs
like Paul Lynde.
Full-bearded Bruce

is a blossoming non-conformist.
Arnold, a mildly bemused Maynard G. Krebs.
I pray
for the gift of facial hair.
Rebels without a clue.

Straw

In '46
David is the first to go away.
I find an empty seat
in desk row three
this warm September day.

In '48
Timmy falls, to rise again
on wooden sticks
and leather straps and iron rods.
He walks like a drunken puppet.

In '51
Bob and Junior rule our city block,
but cannot stop the mournful wind
that rails against the empty fort
behind their parents' house.

In '55
Those of us who still survive
wait in the high school gym.
Balanced between relief and dread,
I feel the needle prick my skin.

In '59
Three thousand miles away,
I stand in yet another gym,

where sounds of life reverberate.
I wait, to drink the bitter draft.
Grateful that I did not draw
the straw
that broke the camel's back,
Belatedly, I say,
"God bless you, Dr. Jonas Salk."

II
Big Muddy

First Date

Two six-year-olds,
skinny legs
dang
  l
    i
      n
       g,
sit on a branch
of the gnarled tree
eating apples.
We watch
the "muddy Mississippi"
roll by.

In my hand,
white pulp
of the half-eaten fruit
glistens.
Tooth tracks furrow the surface.
At the center,
half a worm
  wrig   es.
       ggl

She laughs.
I run home.

John Deere School

No bus came near
the trailer park that stretched itself
along the river bank.
Families pooled their meager funds
to bring the taxi out each day
that carried us to and from
our classes.

Caged in chain-link fence,
on a busy street
in downtown Moline, Illinois.
John Deere School was made of brick,
the color of dirt and ash.
At recess, we played a strange game,
hitting rocks in a box
with sticks.
I cannot, remember why.
When it rained, we came inside
for shuffleboard, in stocking feet.

One day, in first grade class,
I pasted the word "cow"
below the picture of a lamb.
The teacher spanked me with a ruler.
Sometimes, she made us square dance.

River Rat

Tomato red, shaped like bread,
the trailer hunched on the slope
above the river bank.
Twenty-two feet, front to back,
eight feet, side to side,
home for five.

A rat, big as a cat,
it's long tail snapping,
clung to the screen door.
My shoes gave the battle cry
as they hissed through tall grass.
A pointed snout spun my way
to challenge the intrusion.
Our gazes locked
for an instant,
in the ice of mutual fear
and loathing.

I stooped to seize a rock,
felt damp grit beneath my palm.
Muscles bunched, the beast sprang
off to the side yard,
raced to blend into the shadows
at river's edge.

Through the foggy lens

of rusted screen door,
Mother stood facing the kitchen sink
my sister in her arms,
serene, unaware
of my heroic deed.

Mississippi Dip

Feet submerged in muddy water
eyes squeezed to slits
against the afternoon sun,
that hung high
above the distant Iowa shoreline.

Father stood close by,
black hair on white chest,
blue stripes on white swim trunks.
"Walk out to your waist."
No time for negotiation.

One step to the knees,
two steps to the thighs,
three steps to brown darkness.
My hair drifted, in water current.
Bitterness of unsweetened cocoa
filled my mouth,
stung nose, lungs.
Bubbles scurried upward
toward dirty, yellow light.

His huge hand closed
around my upper arm,
lifted me from the hidden hole,
sat me on a flattened rock

until the coughing ceased
and sight returned.
This was to be
our only swimming lesson.

Ralphie

At fourteen, he was forever
seven years old.
All day long,
Ralphie roamed the trailer park,
looking for a friend.

He made a kite for me,
of two-by-fours and newspaper,
a tail of cloth
and a ball of string.

We ran together
across the open field.
Our weighty fledgling bounced, and tumbled
pulled along by twine held taut
in Ralphie's powerful fist.

Where field turned to forest,
we stopped, retraced our steps,
to find the sodden mess
of wood and rag and paper
lying in dew wet grass,
held down
by a trick of nature,
like Ralphie.

III
Panes in Maine

Beach Rose

The little bush stands alone, tenacious, rooted fingers
grasp sandy soil, defy the elements.
Witness to the small ones, abandoned on the rocks, by
fleeing tide, left to die outside their world.
The blossomed, wind-flattened face turns up in
adoration, supplication.
Its fragrance makes this place seem holy.

Mousam River

It flows through the little mill town
of my college years.
In winter, it's a gray-blue highway.
We skate, my friend and I,
to a distant spot of crystal clarity
amidst the opaque.
We see ... rocks, broken branches, a newspaper
beneath our blades.
One quick step back,
and as we flee,
I shudder at what might have been.

In spring, my love and I walk
down to the river,
cross a narrow cement dam
to a grassy outcrop.
She tries to read; I distract
with my harmonica. "Moon River."
Book forgotten, we hold each other
and watch the river push itself
over the small dam in its rush
to the sea,
as the future climbs over the present
to become the past.

Hunters

Each weekday morning in early November,
teenage men
came through the office door
of a rural, twelve-room schoolhouse,
hunters' plaid from head to anklebone.
The night-staled air turned masculine
with gun oil, sweat, and damp wool.

In the principal's office
they laid the rifles, clips removed,
in regimental rows along the table top,
jostled each other down the hall
back into childhood.

At 3 PM the bell released them,
weapons reclaimed, into the dull light
of late autumn afternoon.
They moved with single mind
through parked cars,
across an empty ball field,
slipped through a grate of maple,
oak and ash,
to hunt the families' winter meat.

Flagpole

Teachers stared, over morning cup rims,
out the third floor window,
at the newly-donated flagpole.
Whitewashed, stripped of leaf and limb,
the birch rose to eye level.

Below, students lined the sidewalk,
brought to attention by the old soldier,
survivor of Bataan,
rum blossoms on his cheeks.
He marched four wrinkled Legionnaires
between youthful ranks.

"Present arms!"
Rifles leaped to shoulders.
Gunfire smashed the silence,
rubbing lines of fright on faces
of the younger children.

Eyes followed the smoke stream
up the denuded tree,
past the snapping banner,
to the fresh-sprayed gold
of a toilet ball.

King of the Dump

Tires growl on rough, pebbled asphalt.
Twin yellow center lines lead the way,
slither past forsaken textile mills,
off into stark, sepia landscape
of hardwood forest in late autumn.

Turn right onto pockmarked gravel roadbed
that climbs up and along the ridge.
Gravy colored water sits in potholes,
blossoms outward from beneath the wheels.
Wooden farm gates stand open
beside a faded sign that reads:

  Dump hrs. weekdays 9 AM – 4 PM
          Sat. 9 AM – 12 PM
He stands
at the foot of his mountain,
ready to repel invaders.
Dried mud coats the faded blue coveralls,
boots and undersized hunter's cap.
Legs spread wide, shovel in hand
he gives his Paul Bunyan glare,
as if we had come
to steal his big blue ox.
A finger, yellow with nicotine,
jabs the air.
"Not heyah, ovah theyah!
Don't you people evah lehrn?"

Back in town, he is ignored,
a non-entity to local folk.
But here, amid piles of soggy cardboard,
rotting garbage, flattened beer cans,
rusty appliances
he is a strutting lion
in the court of Oz.
He is King.

Renaissance Maine

On the lawn
a keystone arch
of bald, rubber tires.

Photograph

A pretty woman looks straight ahead,
smiling.
Next to her, the little girl mimics,
holds tightly to mother's hand.
They stand, latest owners,
inside their New England farmhouse
with doors that have latches
and floors of wide, pumpkin pine.

Behind, in front of, passing through them,
a man in worn-out overalls,
his face dragged down in sorrow,
begs for answers with his eyes.
He is trapped between dimensions of time
inside this New England farmhouse
with doors that have latches
and floors of wide, pumpkin pine.

Empathy
(*for Bev*)

When you are in pain,
my aura fades to gray.
Warmth is sucked out of the sun
and rain runs down the window
in my heart.

I try to draw the hurting
from your body, across the room,
and up inside my mind,
roll it into a flaming ball,
will it to my fingertips
and cast the loathsome orb
backward, through time gone by.

I live with this sweet, gentle ache
that comes from constant sharing
of pleasure, pain, loss and gain,
that lasts as long as love itself.

Fort Foster

Wind pushes
restless surf against time-worn rock,
whispers around abandoned battlements,
howls into concrete tunnels,
runs boneless fingers through the hair,
cartwheels a pork pie hat
across the empty parking lot.

Wind pulls
at a corner of discarded sandwich wrap,
that crinkles, softly,
like dry leaves
under a cat's light tread.
Lobster boats purr,
treading water, in the harbor.

Wind ruffles
orange and black monarch wings,
royal blue dragonfly wings,
faded green blades of grass.
The paisley print
of autumn landscape
shivers out of focus,
slow dissolve toward winter.

Wagon Wheel

Three spokes and the hub
lay exposed, sucked clean
by strong, autumn tides.
The rebellious teenager, that was Billy
dragged the intact wheel,
his love offering,
up the steep, muddy bank
to our house.
It stood, rusting red rim
against our old garage.

Raucous voice, cutting wit,
body strength and speedy reflex
armor plates that could not hide
the kindness in his eyes.
Trouble, an excitable pup
tugged at the leash,
pulled him into conflict with authority,
into dark alleys and bar room brawls.

Billy survived it all, with a laugh
that rose from the gut,
and a shake of the head
that sent long hair flying.
Even the wound from a switchblade knife
in a waterfront tavern

couldn't put him down.

There was no chance to survive
the crash of a transport van
carrying oil workers on leave
as it dissolved in flames
on a southern highway.
His laughter faded like thunder
in a distant summer storm.

The wheel was ours for a while
fading from gray to bone.
But as life rolled us away
from the wide salt river,
we left a young boy's simple gift
behind.

Autumn Flight

In October, when the air feels silver,
stand in the yard and listen.
Three-dimensional honking sounds float down
from Canada geese, like feathers in the wind.

Sense the shift in formation.
The lead drops back to rest
in the air stream of the line
and number two moves up into point,
to pierce the endless wall of sky.

As they pass, eavesdrop,
strain to comprehend the conversation
spoken in a language of seasoned migrants…
perhaps they express pity for you,
poor creature
left, landlocked, chained to the rock,
sacrifice to winter's claws.

The arrow shrinks
to a black dot on blue
and its sounds are vacuumed up
into the void.
Pray, fervently, that the birds may, once more,
reach their destination.

Leaf

Death has freed me from the mother.
No more shall I be force-fed
on the bland, sticky sustenance
that flows endlessly
from her vast, lofty storehouse.

Death has broken the chain
that held me, a scapegoat
twisting in the wind
dressed in anonymity
among my countless siblings,
as we struggled to cover mother's nakedness.

In death, I am alive.
Footloose, vibrant with color, I soar,
twist, roll and dive,
drift down to settle
with a feather's touch
into the tapestry of autumn.

Fryeburg Fair

How great it is
to be with Bruce again,
friends since we first rolled up
in our blankets
on the floor, in kindergarten,
so many decades gone by.

We drive, with our wives,
to the fair.
Handicap parking for us these days,
You know it's about
gout and arthritis
and blindness and worn-out parts.
Just a short walk to the draft horse exhibit, where I find you.
Well, not all of you Richard,
just your Cheshire Cat smile,
full of big, white teeth.
You laugh silently, ,
like a little cartoon dog
as patrons dodge falling horse dung.

We walk the gauntlet of craft booths,
stop at a display
of colored, plastic magnetic ribbons bearing slogans
"Support Our Troops" and "Bush – Cheney"
Your smile frowns as you search, in vain, for
"Ban The Bomb."
Then you, Richard, take our hands,
lead us running on youthful feet,

back through night-black, city streets,
to tear the posters down,
from store-front walls and telephone poles,
that evening, just before election day.

The women browse.
We rest on a wooden bench.
"Rollin' in my sweet baby's arms"
The bluegrass band gives us
their best shot.
You sit, across the table,
in that little coffeehouse.
Is it the Insomniac? No, the Iconoclast
down by the beach.
We laugh,
fill our stomachs with cappuccino
our heads with Phil Oaks,
Lenny Bruce, Ferlinghetti.

Time to head for home,
two duffers, swapping memories
as we try to find our car.
What of you, Richard?
You never made it this far,
too soon, you were carried away.
I see your Cheshire smile curl up,
become a crimson leaf, that drops,
swept along,
with broken straws and sandwich wrappers
to God knows where
by an autumn breeze.

May Day

The voices came, while I lay
curled in the thin skin
that held me suspended
during fragile moments of morning sleep.
"Beware, May twenty-six!"
Later, at breakfast,
my wife and her father laugh.
No phantom voice
shall mar the picnic boat ride
planned for this fine May Sunday.

Engines rumbling,
the craft ambles along Sagamore Creek,
muscles out into open water.
One mile to 2KR,
then hard to port and north,
lightly skimming the whitecaps
to the gloss of York Harbor.
At lunch, blue fades
to shades of gray
and the mirrored surface shivers
in anticipation.
The early return of lobster boats
a foreshadowing.

Heading into stiff wind, the bow jumps
at each angry slap,
as we drive a small wedge

through the vast, stampeding waves.
South, finally, we spot the buoy.
A tiny run-about
with four souls stranded there.
Two men, two women,
one rounded with new life,
her frenzied eyes fixed
upon the beckoning figure
who stands on the water
just beyond the reach of our imaginations.

They belong to us
for this wink of time.
Our skipper casts a line,
holds fast,
Sends me, unpracticed, to the wheel.
Focus on Whaleback Light,
first to port
down and up the gray-green trough,
then to starboard.
Back and forth, the lighthouse jumps
across my vision.

Below, our baby sleeps
in the cabin berth.
His mother radios "May Day" in vain,
until pitch and roll defeat her.
Nearby, the silhouette
of a single lobster boat
matches stride, standing vigil,

as we climb, descend and climb again.
Snaking our way across the heaving blanket.
At last, he yells
"Ease back the throttle!"
and strains to hold the lifeline
as we slide gently,
into the mouth of the river
white-faced cargo in tow, intact.

Later, in the slip,
we learn of tragedy to the north.
An overturned boat took many lives.
Only one survived.
Now, there is no laughter
over voices in a dream,
only silence filling the cabin,
and empty glasses on the table.

Lean On Me
(*For Carl*)

From acorn
we worked together,
to push through soil's crust
into sunlight.

Each limb
stretched outward
from Mother trunk,
to touch the sky.

We knew to bend
but not surrender
to nature's winds and whims.

We served;
dropped shade to cool
in summer heat,
dropped leaves to warm
in winter cold.

I stand,
alone now,
but straight and strong
like Mother trunk,
and like the man
who crafts me.

Take hold.
Stand.
Lean on me.

Congress Square

At noon, musicians perform
on the concrete stage
in late spring heat.

Accountants and legal secretaries
sip cappuccino from paper cups.
Shoppers sit with plastic bags
from L. L. Bean and small boutiques
down in the old port.

A homeless man passes by
dressed in Goodwill clothes,
gesticulating wildly
at invisible disciples.

In the Vernacular

Conversation overheard between two locals
having lunch in a small diner,
South Thomaston, Maine:
"The wife made bread yesdiday.
I sliced through it with my knife
whilst the loaf was still hot.
It deflated."
"Mebbe you oughta buy huh
one uh them bicycle pumps."
As we rise to leave
ten minutes later:
"It wuhr nice an dahk too,
not burnt through."

Lobsterman, overheard in the Off Island Market,
Spruce Head, Maine:
"You'd bettah fill thet ice buck-ett
right up to the top,
elst Robeht'uhll shit a twinkie."

Painted Lady Morning

Sun, early in ascent,
warms the air around my face,
as I sit on the porch
of an old, painted lady,
listening.

Perpetual turbines roar,
deep inside the churning surf,
accompanied by irregular hiss and clap
of wave against rock and sand.
Squeals from circling gulls
create an illusion
of rusted wings in flight.

Bits of conversation, laughter,
rise up from passing joggers,
splashes of bright color
on blue-gray slate.

Wind, ragged remnant
of a distant, dying hurricane,
drags itself around the porch
as my chair rocks.
This wind song seems to undulate
in imitation
of restless water beyond the breakers,
a seascape for the ears.

Cornucopia Lost

Gauze of morning frost
coats a pink marble heart
in the cemetery.
Two parallel, grass-covered mounds
stretch outward from the stone,
one, pronounced, newly made,
the other, subtle, settled by time.

Walk away, up the hill.
Look across a country road.
The house is still there,
now occupied by strangers
with lives unknown to you.
Listen in lonely silence.
The breeze carries echoes
of other Thanksgiving days.

Dishes clatter on the family table,
widened by six large oak leaves,
to hold the turkey,
dressing, a myriad of side dishes
and later,
eight different kinds of pie.

Everybody talks at once.
Laughter, uninhibited, flows continuously,
mixes with the tinkling bells

of children's innocent voices.

You wait to catch a glimpse
of the young man you were.
He walks with his sister,
In a time before the pink stone
to the far end of the cemetery
to share a quiet moment.

IV
View from the Zoo

Zoo Keeper

Bird songs kickstart the dawn
as I leave the help's quarters,
taste the salt air,
walk up the driveway
to the outside staircase
at the very back
of the old wooden hotel,
turn left and enter the cafeteria,
known to us as "the zoo".

Rows of long tables with folding chairs
stand as I left them
the night before.
The morning cook, high on something
stirs and smokes.
Gray ash disappears into the oatmeal.

I brew coffee, make the milk:
two parts powdered, one part whole,
two cans condensed.
Set out small triangles of oleo,
little boxes of cereal,
large cans of juice.

Six-thirty brings a reluctant parade....
waitresses in pink,
bellhops in white and green,
chambermaids and kitchen helpers

Mike Rogers

some with eyes puffed
from youthful, summer debauchery.
The maintenance crew, skid row men
suffering sobriety just long enough
to earn another ride on the slide.

The room fills
with the sounds of muffled conversation
and scraping of utensils on crockery.
Smells of bacon fat,
coffee, cigarette smoke,
perfume and after-shave.
Chairs carom into tables, as workers leave
to find a slot in the day.

I pick up the pieces....
refrigerate, empty, put away, sweep,
wash down table tops
with toxic cleaning fluid.
Then, leave the zoo
and enter the real kitchen.
to hunt, stalk, steal my breakfast.
Do the pretty people out front
think of us as beasts?

Big Red

Summer drew him, a lemming,
to the big hotel
at the edge of the sea.
Knight of the road
without damsel, horse or quest.
His W-4 read: "Main Street, U.S.A."

Six feet plus he loomed.
A frizzy ring of monkish hair
wrapped the back of his head,
thick mats of copper thread
shielded his freckled forearms,
proclaimed his moniker.
Bent, round, wire-rimmed glasses
crouched on plastic feet
atop a pug nose.
Small, widely-spaced, yellowed teeth
lined his smile.

Walloping pots in the big stainless sink,
his stance
defied all pretenders to the throne.
A no-nonsense man submerged in his calling.
During breaks, the yarn spinner regaled us
with tales of kitchen intrigue
from across the land
in times gone by.
It was his life, his justification.

The menthol cigarette,
phoenix rising from between his lips,
a constant companion.
Each inhalation a grimace,
followed by expulsion
through puffed cheeks and pouted mouth ...
Father Wind
propelling ancient, striped sail-clad vessels
across a storybook cover.
He built an image
with three packs a day.
Smoke rings drifted up between us,
separating man from child.
His laughter choked, threatened to drown him.

In the fall, he would slip away,
unnoticed
to the other coast;
Flotsam, caught in the rainbow current
of an oil-slicked puddle.

A Cruel Cut

He drops his kitchen uniform
on the bed.
Gray work pants and once-white t-shirt
stained with sweat, dirty dish water, food.
Into the communal shower room,
He smiles at the face
in the foggy mirror.
Covers the tiny cut with toilet paper.

Splash on a palm full
of Old Spice cologne.
He bought it yesterday.
Spit-shine the well-scarred black dress shoes.
Button the new white shirt
with French cuffs.
Red tie,
to go with the dark blue suit,
custom cut.
He wore it to his mother's funeral.

Down the stairs, out the door
to the canteen,
next to the help's dormitory.
Waits on the porch steps.
Cuts his eyes to the women's quarters
across the parking lot.

It's a date. The first,
in his forty-eight years.

A blind date.
Set up
by the tall, skinny bellhop.
"She really digs you, Red."
Odd, this sudden act of friendship.
What will he say,
when she shows up?
"Hey doll,
I'm the guy you're lookin' for.."
He's going for that "Bogie" image.
Not one to waste words.
Cut to the chase.

Kids on the way to evening shift,
glance his way.
Is it curiosity... or something else?
Never look them in the eye.
Just a cut above the rest.

Shoot the cuff. Check the Bulova.
She's late.
Thirty minutes,
he rubs the toe of his shoe
against the back of his pant leg.
At hour's end, he knows.
She's not coming.
There is no "she."
A joke.
Laughter, from an open window
cuts to the quick.

Canned Heat

Dim light from a 60 watt bulb
casts sharp shadow lines
across a dirty concrete floor
in the dormitory bathroom.

Wilbur keeps his thick, white hair
trimmed and carefully combed.
Distinguished, horn-rimmed glasses
fail to hide blood-shot eyes
that peer from a face
as wrinkled as the paper bag
that holds the stolen can of sterno.

Liver-spotted hands shake with deprivation,
scoop wax from the container,
wrap it in cheese cloth,
squeeze and squeeze again,
until raw, alcoholic poison
drips into the glass of cola.

Steady now, use both hands
bring it safely to the lips,
knock it back, drive the dragons,
memories of a life destroyed,
back into their cave.
Fire burns upward from the bowel,
slows trembling in the limbs.

He turns to the mop and bucket
that wait, like a summoned taxi,
to carry him
to his next real drink.

Magician

His little sink sat sacrosanct,
in the rear right corner
of the kitchen in the old resort.
Herbie washed and polished every piece:
each silver knife, fork, spoon,
each sterling ice cream dish
until it gleamed in bloodless fluorescent light.

This frail guardian of the Holy Grail,
in short-sleeved shirts of army green,
stood his watch in two hotels,
north in summer breezes,
south in winter sun.
Each working day, a repeat performance,
allowed no time, gave no permission
to color outside the lines.

Only sunlight through the corner window
shining on his sunken cheeks,
brought him comfort.
"I'm invisible. Can you see me?"
We played along, humored him.
"Where's Herbie? He's gone!"
He would laugh every time.

The *maître de* often used him
for the focal point of jokes,
as impotent bullies often do.

One day,
the joke was not so funny.
Herbie ripped a counter gate
screws and all, from off its hinges.
He chased the bug-eyed big man
through heavy double doors
into the forbidden world
of crystal chandeliers
and linen tablecloths.

Orange light filled the sky
one night as the dormitory burned.
Like a mouse on the run,
Herbie darted through flickering shadows,
around the noise-filled parking lot
skirted knots of sleepy hotel staff,
who stood and spoke with quiet voices.
Then he turned, broke and ran
past ranks of helmeted firefighters.
Silhouetted black in the yellow doorway,
Herbie gave his last performance,
disappearing forever.

V
Island Time

Christoforo

Who was this man, Christoforo?
Son of a woolweaver, standing proud,
the longboat glides over brilliant reef.
Boots splash through the surf,
cross coral sand into prickly grass.
He greets the smiling innocents,
jams his standard
down between their naked feet,
deems them worthy to be slaves.

His triad brings a song of sorrow
heard throughout the island chain,
siphons off all life and dignity,
leaving only echoes
to host the bands of pirates
yet unborn.

Who was this man, Christoforo?
Navigator extraordinaire? Saint? Savior?
Father of a continent?
Or little man whose boot-heels betrayed him
as he stood
atop his hill of human bones,
sent him tumbling, dragged by chains
into a Spanish dungeon?

A wooden carving of his face
stares out

above the door, on an island church…
at a dazzling Caribbean seascape,
as governments declare a holiday
one day each year
in honor of his misdeeds.

Witch Baby

People warned us of this little demon.
In the bush along the roadside,
it crouches, hiding in the dark,
watching the incautious traveler.

Those who wait to walk in twilight,
need a sturdy stick at hand,
to ward off this hoodoo creature,
drive it back to the conjuror.

Midnight's gloom
chased us through the abandoned schoolyard
toward our home, a crumbling barracks.
A violent screech, rising from the right,
caused frightened flesh to shinny
up my spine,
cling fiercely to my neck,
tighten over my skull.

Above the angry pounding
of surf on rock,
a slow flap of heavy wings
lifted the goulding, island scavenger
off on some nocturnal quest.
Definitely not a witch baby.

Bahama Nights

Uninterrupted sleep is fantasy
in the little house of sounds…
scratch of sand crab claws
on rotten clapboards…
Whispered flutter of flying roach,
that lands, rests,
gnaws on naked flesh,
while wingless cousins crunch
dry food in kitty's dish…
The flimsy ceiling creaks
 under footfalls of approaching rat…
Rat-tat tattoo of rat tail
on tiled floor,
but the cat offers no quarter…
crow of rooster, coo of dove
announces blessed daylight.

Island Road

We ride the narrow band.
Twenty-four miles it circles,
swallowing it's own tail.
I feel the tropic sun press down,
to be brushed aside
by ever-present trade winds.

Our bicycle tires purr,
Bouncing on soft, blacktop …
rhythmic pounding of surf
on sand and rock
dry rustle of palm fronds
in the breeze.

The air smells alternately sweet and sour:
of flowers, rotting vegetation…
of salt water, bait…
of vitality, corruption.

House on Fox Hill

It sits leaning
into the side of the small hill,
A rear guard
holding back the Island bush
from overrunning Cockburn Town.
A black-top tide of narrow road
edges close to cement steps
of an open porch.

Lifting padlock from hasp,
we pull open the front door
and push our way
through inner screen to darkness and heat.
Top hinged shutters lay dropped over glassless windows.
Thin strips of turquoise daylight
underline clapboards, where termites have devoured
all but the outer layer of paint.

Our noses wrinkle,
at the assault from mold
rotten wood, dirt, stale air and clothing
left in closets these five years.

Twenty feet from front to back,
fifteen from side to side. Four rooms with walls
open at the top.
Step down into the galley kitchen,
bedroom to the right.

To the left, a back door.
An outdoor faucet is mounted
over a sinkless counter.

All around us, winged and crawling,
nature's scavengers scratch at the silence.
On the beam above our heads
a long tail curls and slaps
against wood.
 hostile eyes order us to leave.

Startled, we retreat to the front entrance,
out into sweet relief,
and fill our lungs.
We must, somehow,
make this into our home.

Night Drop

Rough tracks jolted the borrowed van
into the bush,
past disintegrating slave quarters
of a vanished plantation,
during midday heat of a Caribbean summer.

A faded shirt on rusty hanger
marked hidden wheel-ruts
that beckoned likecrooked fingers
up the short, steep incline
to a sunlit knoll.
All vegetation cleared by hand,
the earthen eye stared skyward.
Listening, we heard danger,
in the silence.

At home that night,
sound slapped us awake.
Two hundred feet aloft,
a cargo–laden DC-3
rumbled over ... surf and rock,
shuttered windows,
a darkened island airstrip,
a headlight-brightened patch of ground,
then, gone.

As heartbeats slowed,
we wondered If our own silence
made us guilty of conspiracy.

VI
Mason Dixon

Bell Ringer

December sun spreads diluted warmth
over a sparse audience
gathered in the bank parking lot,
where a Baptist choir gives tribute
to the birth of the Messiah.

Scuff of leather soles on sidewalk cement
effluvium of moldy clothing
announce the new arrival at my elbow.

He is big, and bald,
with eyes that pin you
like a bug to a card.
Pink Bermuda shorts over sagging slacks
ride low on the hips.
Two dress shirts trap the body heat.
Around his neck, a copper cowbell
hangs from a once-white string.

Hands, chafed by cold,
grip the plastic bag
that holsters his dreams and paranoia
disability applications in soiled envelopes,
two honed butcher knives,
38 caliber pistol,
tattered copy of *The Holy Bible*.

His deep voice rings,
like the clapper in his bell,
denouncing welfare injustice,

drug addicts in the neighborhood,
Godlessness in the world.
He claims a damaged spine
but the real wound lies deep inside.

His ailing mother will have no Christmas.
Can I help?
Having been born yesterday, I oblige.
With a ferret's swiftness,
he spins to face a passing shopper
who has failed to look away
in time.

For a Pear

The morning heat is tolerable
this Georgia summer day.
We stand beneath the outer circle of leaves
and I hold tight
to the flimsy aluminum ladder.

Morgan's sneakered foot mounts the bottom rung
launches the shaky ascent on legs
ravaged long ago by childhood disease.
With each climbing step, the ladder sways
from side to side, a living thing
bearing weight upon its shoulders.

Standing on top rung,
Morgan grabs a branch for balance,
stretches a long arm toward the prize.
A pear, big as a softball,
sways its hips teasingly
just above his fingertips.
Up on tiptoe, lunge, grasp, and pull.

The fragile stem resists, then too soon
relinquishes all ties with the tree mother.
Eluding groping fingers, the liberated fruit
rockets downward,
a hawk dropping on a field mouse,
punches a tunnel through layers of living leaves,
through space.

I hear his warning cry too late.
The rock hard missile greets the bridge
of my nose.
A cracking, squishing sound reverberates
around the interior of my skull.
Pain liquefies my eyes.
In a speck of time, my appearance is
slightly, but irrevocably altered.

Sunnyland or Bust

"Can you help me get to Florida?
I'm a little down on my luck."
Her face was lined with highway miles.
Blonde hair, going gray, hung unwashed,
pointing downward
at second-hand attire.

We sat on plastic chairs
inside the Dairy Queen
looking up at her.
My wife stood, walked to the counter,
ordered a burger, fries, Coke,
offered them to the sojourner
who accepted unwanted gifts,
with sullen eyes.

One year later …
we walked to our car
in the mall parking lot.
The road-weary face turned our way.
"Can you help me
get to Florida?
I'm a little down on my luck."

Different Worlds

Small blonde heads bob
in water warmed by summer sun.
Pale hands splash crystal droplets
that quickly evaporate on the decking.
Pale faces share knowing smiles.

Outside the tall chain-link fence,
children of color stand barefoot
on the hard-packed, red clay road.
They stare,
from the corners of their eyes,
at the "public" swimming pool
in the little southern town.
Not everyone shares Martin's dream.

Family Matter

In pre-dawn darkness, the engine screams,
harbinger of drunken rage.
He stomps the accelerator to the floorboard,
holding the big Olds motionless,
in the driveway.

Across the road, I jack-knife
out of dreamless sleep.
My heart slams against the bars
of its bony cage.

In morning sunlight, his wife limps
around piles of empty beer cans,
to the roadside.
Her shuffling footsteps whisper
of brutality long endured.

At noon, their son returns.
A watchman's pistol hangs from his belt.
His father sits in the bedroom,
surrounded by a private arsenal.

Angry threats burst through open windows.
Cicada check their summer drone,
momentarily shouted down
by the roar of gunfire.
The elder figure slumps to the floor.
Blood soaks the unswept boards.

Self defense, no charges filed.

VII
Music Goes Round and Round

If You Had Seen Just What I Heard

Sonny Terry

You would never remember me.
We spoke, some thirty years ago,
in the old gymnasium
of that small, New England college,
during your sound check.
We were both blind harmonica players.
You were my idol.

My mind drifts back to the sixties.
I watch, through younger eyes,
as you play the blues
on Pete Seeger's TV show.
With one minute left in the program,
you explain your technique.
My life, irrevocably altered.

You become the focus of my ambition.
I study your "riffs," your "glisses,"
the deep richness of your single notes,
rhythms that fill me with joy,
like a dog turned loose
to run through tall grass.
I strive to become you,
in time, to become others.
Finally,
I become me.

Your stage is empty now.
The plaintive wailing of your southern harp

echoes from my stereo.
On my stage,
I bend the notes and drive rhythms
into the core of each listener
and wait to pass
into that new dimension
where I may meet you again
and say, "Thanks."

In the Zone
(for J.P.)

Elusive, seductive, addictive,
performers sweat, die to get there.
First high, little death.

In the zone …
you are one with the audience.
Captives of a wizard spell
struggle vainly to remain
inside the moment.

In the zone …
practiced voices align,
flow into thirsty ears.
Two instruments form
a carillon …
a driving wheel.

Later, on the other side
memory hears, sees, tastes …
stretches to regain,
but cannot touch
The Zone.

Music Man
(for Phil)

Every week, he rode the circuit,
three thousand songs stacked in his head.
He tossed them out to the spectators
at his parade.

On tour with Armstrong in the sixties,
until love of family drew him
back inside the circle.
His voice brushed color
over shadows on the mountainside,
brought back life to tired minds
of old ones in the valley.

Three days, we blended, harmonized,
at his hillside home
and in a smoky, restaurant bar
high up on the summit.
I gathered tunes by the armful,
so many that some slipped away.

We talked about more sessions
but, suddenly, the music turned to stone
on a twisting Sierra highway.
No longer do fingers press the neck
of that big, six-string guitar.
I have stacked the songs he gave me
just behind the door inside my memory.

Audition
(for Barbara)

She slides clothes hangers along the rod,
blue or beige, print or plain?
Settle for basic black, with simple lines,
Low heeled shoes.
One last check
in the full-length mirror.

Behind the wheel, meditative breathing,
in through the nose, out through the mouth..
So many years since this was necessary,
but her chops are together.
She is ready.

In the lounge, she shakes Sid's hand.
He has capped teeth and plastic hair.
He is the manager.
She asks, "What are you looking for?"
He glances past her right ear,
answers through his nose, "Somebody attractive."

From the piano bench, she watches.
Sid dissolves, like Houdini into the cosmos.
Play now, as for Paganini.
Cause the lounge lizards to flip,
kicking their legs in the air.

A waitress from the next room
appears at her side.
Dining patrons complain about the volume.
The bench bites into her buttocks.
Inside her head, steel doors slam shut.
Suddenly, the long-dreamed-about Hawaiian vacation
looms large.

First Night 2000

In the city square, floodlights
cast the sculpture in gold.
Ice horses drag their chariot
into the twenty-first century.
Inside the Old South Church
that was our stage,
volunteers search under every seat
for suspicious bags left unattended.

Four jobs, four audiences,
we stow the tired instruments
in our old Honda wagon
and walk across the street
to the grassy slope
at the edge of the pond.

Gyrating on a flatbed stage,
Elvis, dressed in white, is risen.
He closes with "Dixie",
"Battle Hymn of the Republic"
and the countdown begins.
Explosions shake brilliant colors
into the night.
Cold air shakes the flesh
on my bones.
But I am content.
New Year's day is here
without the threatened bombs.

Mistake

We're in the pocket.
The audience hangs on every word,
every note.
I pull vibrato from the big chromatic,
the sound so sweet,
it makes my eyes sweat.
Our instruments descend from minor to major seven,
drop to root, ascend to the five.
Hold for two measures ...
Where's the band?
There's one more verse.
Damn!

The competition is over for us.
No!
I begin to sing *a capella*.
They can follow or leave me hanging.
Buddy's guitar eases In,
Joe's snare snaps, bass drum kicks.
They're back.

Two songs, and we're done.
The crowd gives a standing "o"
and we've won!
Backstage, they say, "It Works.
Use it."

Sittin' In

Noise snaps at us
through the open windows
as we cross the parking lot.
A plywood ramp
brings us to the front door,
into smoke and beer smell and testosterone.
I order ginger ale,
get Sprite in a plastic cup.
The band plays oldies,
too new for me to recognize.

To the stage, invited I stand
at the microphone,
silhouetted before Ted Turner's face
as he grins out
from the sports channel.
We launch into some Led Zeppelin,
amplification shredding my mastoids
and libido.

Three songs, and I'm out the door.
Through it all,
my father sits at home,
watching forty-year-old reruns
of Lawrence Welk.
This night,
the span of years that holds us
at constant points of separation,
has diminished.

Through a Glass Darkly

The closing song echoes in the room.
Our listeners walk, shuffle,
are wheeled back to semi-private lives.
The taste of chocolate
lingers in each mouth.

The trio packs up instruments.
A voice at my elbow drifts up
through cotton clouds
of confusion and advanced years.
I ask him to repeat himself,
search the pile for missing pieces
to his question.

"Yes, harmonicas," I say,
"Each one, a different key."
I hope
that this is what he asks.
He talks of accordions,
pipe organs, church
and asks his question three times more.

Two times, I give my answer,
then tell him that we must leave.
It is my wish
to find him well.
I know, when we return,
That he will hear me again,
for the first time.

VIII
Outside the Circle

Otto

Nobody knew where Otto lived…
his family, his job, his dreams.
Frightened child in a man's body.

His gaze never strayed from the space
just above the handlebars
of his bicycle.
Feet encased in brown scuffed wingtips,
perpetually pedaled.

Sometimes, prone in tall grass
at the side of the road,
he would stare across the gully.
Green pants, green shirt, the Texaco man
camouflaged in the weeds, riding point
for some invisible platoon.

Two eyes, widened by life's surprises,
watched, unblinking, from the middle
of a wrinkled infant face,
a tableau known to him alone.

Otto rides down every street,
ancient bike clattering over bumps and potholes.
He sits on deserted bus-stop benches,
peeks through sun-dried blades
in vacant lots and roadside fields.
Everyone has seen him…
seen right through him…
looked away.

Acrobat Man

Summer 1956 on Sapphire Street beach
he makes his way
down the cement stairway.
Tanned and wrinkled, not very tall
his bald head glows in summer sun.
A faithful audience,
adolescents perched
on brightly colored beach towels,
watch his entrance.

At water's edge, where sand packs hard
he stands, rooted,
with eyes fixed on the sky.
Snap the body backward
into the air,
knees tucked up under ribs
spin, tumble through space …
descend, legs uncoil to absorb shock.
Sand crystals, displaced
by the soles of his feet,
sparkle as he steadies himself.

Shoulders hunched, he exits the stage
with a sailor's rolling gait.
Reliable as the tide,
he will be here tomorrow.

Like royalty, he ascends the steep steps
that lead to Sapphire Street.

Ouida

"Ouida has cooties!"
Every day they chanted,
plucked at her sleeve
with fingers covered by folded paper,
little white boxes that opened
to reveal black dots made with crayon.
Smiling through tears, she gave chase
across the playground.

At seven, Ouida dwarfed the others.
Black, bowl-cut hair, a cap
over pale, fleshy features
that seemed to float
above the flower print tent dress
and black tie shoes,
that was her uniform.

She was the sideshow
in an empty row of desks
joined front to back
on wooden runners.

When school let out in June,
she disappeared, to grow, to soar
like a swan with graceful wings,
above her tormentors,
or fall, crushed beneath the feet
of mean, little people.

Taboo

What could have possessed him?
Caught doing what adolescents do,
in a locker room stall
by a football coach, of all people.
Caught red handed,
and the school term just beginning

For three years he was doomed
to walk, friendless, through the hallways,
to hear the knowing whispers,
"Here comes ------.
He's the one who ..."

You saw him rarely,
a solitary silhouette
outlined against distant buildings,
or trudging home, along the sidewalk
with eyes cast down, searching
for his lost sense of worth.

As the mind leapfrogs over decades
to watch him pass by,
you ask yourself:
"What if it wasn't true?
And what did it matter, anyway?"

Star on Loan

Each day that winter week
the Yellow Cab dropped us
on Park Avenue,
near the St. Regis Hotel.
Up three steps
into the warmth of Paul's Food.
The table, always empty
rested just inside the door.

She waited on us every time,
in her nearly clean, green uniform.
Two eggs over easy
toast and coffee.

On Friday, our last day there,
She spoke:
"Are you guys musicians?
I'm a singer myself.
This job is only temporary
you know, between engagements."

"Ever heard of Janis Joplin?
Seen how she holds it?"
Her hand raised the invisible microphone,
tilted it downward
to an upturned mouth.
"I taught her that."

In His Eyes

In adolescence
his stare could cast daggers
into your safe place.
Adults would feel enfeebled by his presence.

The eyes were pieces of winter sky.
Sometimes he would smile,
but his gaze lay
suspended in a bitter pool.
To attempt a glimpse inside
was to rattle a locked door.

He toyed with weakness, batting it
here and there before the final strike,
gratification astride the back
of induced suffering.

Now, the eyes burn holes
through steel doors
that separate him from freedom.
They are eyes devoid of compassion
or remorse,
for violent acts committed.

Uptown Threads

"Looking good!"
said the spiky-haired young man
in his orange pants
with matching Hawaiian shirt.

He walked along State Street,
snapping his fingers
to the tune in his head.

Vision of Loveliness

Just inside the box store door
an elderly woman
wrapped in lavender
yodels
like a Nashville pro.

Just a Closer Walk

Black against florescent pink sunset,
the figure moves in silhouette
along the shoulder of the road,
west of town.
The stride is long, military,
never, altered.
He walks, has walked this route
each day for decades.

Closer now, illumined by twilight,
see how the long pheasant quill
fastened to his snap-brim cap
bows and waves with every step.
Tweed jacket with leather elbow patches,
jeans, sensible shoes,
his face, a marble fortress.

"Happy young fellah, never a problem"
that's what folks say.
This, before the government picked him up,
dropped him in an Asian jungle,
a land of thatched roof huts,
to hunt and kill an elusive enemy.

Do not bother with greetings,
as he passes your front yard.
This victim of a long gone war
has no desire to see you,

know you, know about you.
His glare spikes the horizon,
where something lost dances
through shades of green and brown,
and black.

Stick Man

At morning rush hour
in downtown Manhattan,
you stare through a break
in pedestrian traffic.

The man in camouflage clothes
beats an empty Marlboro box
with a broken broom handle.
Over and over and over,
he flattens
the tiny red and white container
on the damp sidewalk.
Corded muscles outline the jaw
and underscore eyes that glare
at demons that cavort
behind your left shoulder.
His lips disappear, exposing teeth
that push against each other.

Across the six-lane avenue,
gaze fixed straight ahead,
a famous newscaster
strides purposefully
toward an unseen studio
far above the hoi polloi.

IX
Sunset

Evening Ritual

"Time for bed," you coax.
"I'll be in
when you're ready for me."
Upstairs, I listen for his call
and the rumble of his walker
over linoleum in the hall.

He sits
on the closed-down toilet seat.
I gently pull the shirt
up over his head.
Bristled whiskers, .
wispy curls brush my arm
On with the pajamas, button by button.
Follow his wheels down the hall,
into the bedroom.

Pull back the blankets,
but he gets in by himself.
Covers tucked in tight,
little pillow placed just so,
"Down, more to the right.
There."
Give the hug, feel the fear.
Say the words of love
both of us need to hear
so desperately.

Leave the door open, just a crack.
Climb the carpeted stairs.
Remember Wordsworth's line
that stayed with me through college years,
Now blurred in memory's vision.
"The child is father of the man."

Hourglass

In the emergency room again,
with windowless walls and mechanical sounds
that pulse and sigh and measure,
I sit with him, and wait.

Through the lens of time, I see
a powerful fist, with pointing finger
that could hold me immobile,
the ruddy face with flashing eyes,
that manifested absolute authority.

In the house, dust lies,
like dandruff on the shoulder,
over projects started long ago,
dreams that wait to become trash.
Christmas cards lay cupboard,
piled on the Hoosier
wait for him to decide their fate.

The safety net has been dismantled.
He walks a rope on shaking legs.
I hold tight to his hand,
But cannot hold him upright.

Vigil

She is there again tonight,
out of reach, beyond the bed,
a wonderful, expensive bed
that gently lifts the knees, feet, head.
Her long, white dress is made of light
that soothes the gritty sting
inside his thirsty eyes.

This is not the face
he looked into, one last time,
before the undulating vital sign
flattened out along the monitor screen
four lonely, bone-tired years ago.

This face once smiled at him
across a dime store lunch counter.
He sat, in U.S. Navy blues,
asking for her hand in marriage,
while Adolf Hitler tried in vain
to burn their world down.

She looks, but does not see
the withered husk that houses him.
She sees, instead, her sailor boy
with curly hair and flashing eyes,
dressed in white light.
There are no words between them,
but now he knows
she waits,
for him alone.

Year of the Orphan

Alone? Not really.
But when the last aging parent dies
you wake one morning,
a step ahead of first light,
with that gut-punched feeling
of abandonment.

"The number you are dialing
has been disconnected."
Their house is gone, sold,
disguised in fresh paint, wallpaper, carpet.
Possessions, those treasured,
divided among survivors,
the rest, purchased for a song
by strangers, seeking their own treasure.

Memory, a separate world,
is where you journey
to reminisce, seek approval,
 lament, beg forgiveness,
look for answers.

Nothing for it now
but to push reluctant feet
into deserted shoes.
You, orphan
have become the elder.

X
Snapshots

One-Line Poems

Tandem Cycling
The back-pedaler can never steer you wrong.

Migrant Birds Over A Cathedral
Honk if you love Jesus.

Braille On The A.T.M.
Driving there is half the battle.

Winning the Lottery
Keep a snowflake in your pocket.

Gross Neglect
How many dozen times must this happen?

National Security
"Boxers, when flying, please check fists
at the gate."

TV Reality Shows
An exciting, new season of evenings,
spent avoiding reality.

Free Performance
This makes no cents.

Enigma

In the Bronx,
there is a driving range
snug against the I-95 expressway,
island of green
in a sea of dirty brick brown.

The net rises forty feet
above a river of traffic,
spans the range from side to side,
a thin skin to absorb tiny white missiles
that have overshot the mark.

You! Driver! Yes, you!
Look up,
in the right quadrant of your windshield
There! Twenty feet up
directly in the center of the net,
the tiny figure clings,
like a spider in his web.
Wide eyes stare
at the rushing madness below.
Square pants quiver in the wind.

Do you see it?
Sponge Bob!
How on earth ... ?

Jerusalem Swings

A prostitute stands in the road
that overlooks this Turkish marketplace.
One stiletto-heeled foot rests
atop the low fender
of a little red sports car.
Her leather mini skirt rides high.
Lips move and hands gesture
as she negotiates.

Five smiling, middle-aged Americans
walk past the trick in progress.
They wear matching, blue sweatshirts,
with white footprints, and the words:
"I Walked Where Jesus Walked!"

Below, we wait on steps
that slope steeply between rows of stalls,
where merchants display prayer rugs, jewelry,
rose candy, K-Mart dresses.

Our backs are turned to the crowd
that presses unceremoniously past, in descent.
A stealthy finger slides, almost unnoticed,
into the back pocket of my jeans,
discovers the soiled handkerchief,
retreats.

At noon, the pre-recorded call to prayer

rattles from a suspended loudspeaker.
As sellers close their stalls,
one approaches with a prayer rug.
"Too much." We tell him,
turn to climb the stairs.
He follows, drops the price
at each upward step
We slow, turn back, haggle, purchase
and hurry to the waiting tour van
with flowers painted on the doors.

Down to Galilee

Paper plates of strawberries and dates
lay before us on the table.
Remnants of ancient Tiberius surround the patio,
scalloped columns and chunks of broken marble,
scattered twigs and pieces of bark
dropped from a giant, petrified tree
in a mighty storm.

I chip my tooth on an unforgiving pit
as we eat, in pale sunlight.
We rise and walk the beach,
stop to touch a sculpted pillar.
From shallow water,
we pluck small, rounded stones,
slippery, like this obstinate land,
too slippery for an empire's hand.

Before a Fall

On these mornings, I wake,
stare at the blind spot
in my memory.
Pain hunches low in my abdomen,
then springs up into the hole
just behind my eyes.
Nausea swims on my tongue.

As I rise from bed,
the load inside my head shifts, settles.
To the bathroom
On boneless legs
to empty out last night's venom.
"Please, God, help me through this
and I promise………"

Down the stairs, white knuckles,
on the rail
I leave the innocents asleep.
In the kitchen, the jug sits patiently,
half-empty, never half-full.
Find the biggest tumbler.

Move to the sun porch,
Chianti quivers in my shaking hand.
Morning light sparkles on the river,
white-hot shards of glass.
The body sits and the mind stands

teetering on the edge of the eye socket.
"Jump!" I scream.

The red wine flows,
pushes back the pain,
eases the nausea, nods encouragingly.
The world focuses; I light a cigarette.
I'm back. I'm in control....
or something is.

Lost in Space

At night in the darkened bedroom,
waiting for sleep to unbuckle restraints
that hold me captive
in a chaotic day,
I launch my mind.

It punches through the ceiling,
into blackness pinpricked with white,
roaring soundlessly past constellations,
a million billion miles
to newly discovered galaxies.

In this windless vacuum
I wonder, for an instant,
if our universe is flat
and I will sail off the edge.

Made in the USA
Middletown, DE
27 June 2023